side covers: Draft of the original
381 constitution of the Waifs and Strays—
er the Church of England Children's
ciety—in the hand of its founder, Mr, later
ebendary, Edward Rudolf.

Children First

A PHOTO-HISTORY OF ENGLAND'S CHILDREN IN NEED

Written and compiled by

BILL BOWDER

for the Church of England Children's Society

1881–1981

MOWBRAY   LONDON & OXFORD

Preface

by Sir John Betjeman CBE

An infant crying in the night:
An infant crying for the light:
And with no language but a cry.

TENNYSON

This is the story of the Waifs and Strays, now called the Church of England Children's Society.

This book is wanted. It is readable and informative and sometimes funny. Its pictures are genuine and often touching. It shows that a great deal of work is done which is unofficial and useful. It is about people and it is not written in the meaningless jargon used by so many social workers.

JOHN BETJEMAN

Contents

Introduction

For a hundred years and more children have been taken from their homes, their relatives, their friends and their old haunts to be brought up with strangers. This is the story of some of those children, many of whom lost everything to start a new life in the Homes and foster families of the Church of England Children's Society. Hundreds of thousands of them were in need of the very basic necessities of life—warmth and food, someone who cared for them, a roof over their heads. They were the often forgotten legacy of a century of social unrest, war, poverty, disease, parental cruelty and death. This is their tale, told in a unique photo-record drawn from those years. The photographs, which cast a dramatic light on the conditions in which those 'forgotten children' lived are complemented by their personal reminiscences and those of the men and women who looked after them and helped to make up this fascinating chapter in the history of England.

CHAPTER 1

Endings and beginnings

Above: A child apparently trying to get into the Children's Society's headquarters in Kennington, London. The picture is 1913 and the child is comparatively well off, note his shoes, cap and strong clothes. He does not seem in need of rescue.

Left: Three ragged children around the year 1890. Frequently the older child was left to look after the younger children while mother was out finding work and father, all too often, was drowning the sorrows of the slums in cheap alcohol.

A boy lay asleep on his hard bed. He was eleven years old and had had enough. London's teeming slums waited for him outside. His friends would be kipping under carts or on doorsteps tonight for it was a warm evening. But he was through with running, running from his father's beatings, running from the law. Here, in the casual ward of the vast infirmary, built to house several thousand, there was a kind of haven. An old man was coughing. Earlier the boy had thought he had found a friend, but he did not want that kind of attention. Too many of his mates had turned to selling themselves. Angrily he rejected the man's advances. The ward was settling down. The boy dared to relax and soon he was breathing gently, dreaming he had food to eat and fine clothes to wear.

It was after midnight when the Rector and the Reverend Charles Whitaker called at the infirmary. The Rector was a Poor Law guardian and as he studied the dissipate prematurely aged faces of the thirty-five men in the ward his eye took in the youth and innocence of the lad asleep. 'Send that lad to me at ten o'clock tomorrow morning,' he instructed the infirmary official who accompanied them. 'I will see what can be done for him.'

Charles Whitaker knew he could not help—the night before on another rescue mission he had found four candidates for the vacancies in his own children's home at Natland in Cumbria. There seemed no end to the distressing sights of destitute children, and so few places for them to go where they would grow with any semblance of a decent life. But now, at least, one more child was on the road to rescue. What did it mean to a lad, knee high to a grasshopper, who had never been a mile from the slum of his birth, scratched when he felt like it and swore like hell, to be dragged in front of a black-coated cleric? The Law and the Church. It was all the same to him. Big men asking prying questions. Give them a straight answer and your dad would flay the skin off your back if he ever got to hear of it. Tell a lie and these gents were not above turning the law onto you.

Who knew what was behind the smiling face of this stranger and his offer of a new home? The street beckoned. The stench, the drunkenness, fighting, the noise of strange men on the stairs as mother hustled him and his brother out of the way. All this was familiar. The man promised a new life, another chance—and he promised a full belly. It was enough, he would risk going with his rescuer.

It was one of the hazards of street life in the late 1800s, being rescued. The stories that came back of life in the Homes kept many a lad glancing over his shoulder lest he became the next to be saved. Crammed into uniform, ordered about, set to work, cut off from your friends, the Homes had a bad reputation on the streets.

The army of philanthropists, deeply shocked at what they saw when they penetrated behind the fashionable areas of the metropolis, had little time for such scruples of childhood. To them the slums were the hot bed of evil and disease and degradation—Satan's own lair on earth. To men and women reared in the power and wealth of late Victorian England the answer to such evils was a clean break, an end to the old life and a new beginning for those souls they could find and rescue.

Under the leadership of a Cavalry officer's son the Church set out to rescue its own. The Waifs and Strays Society, formed in 1881 was unabashed in its aim—to make sure that destitute children were reared in the teachings of the established church. It was a time when religious brand loyalty was at its height and empire building was not confined to overseas—the established church wanted its own empire in child care.

The power and influence of the Church of England was enormous, as befitted an imperial church. Once the waifs and strays scheme received the blessing of the Archbishop of Canterbury, Dr. Tait, the work exploded into action. Children poured in, recommended by vicars throughout the country who were all too reluctant to place orphans within the grim Poor Law establishments and who had no money to pay the price of private care. Donations flooded in, even whole houses were given and in every parish the vicar spread the news and appealed to the God-fearing for support.

The meteoric expansion held dangers for the freedom-loving children of the streets. For while the founder of the Waifs and Strays, Edward Rudolf, seems to have had a natural understanding of the needs of children, his society was busy taking over existing Homes which were deeply steeped in a tradition of harsh discipline. Such a Home may have started under the inspired leadership of a genuine philanthropist, but he had gone long since and the trustees he had left to continue the work were all too often people with little interest and less love for the children.

It all depended on the house committees which ran the Homes. If they were tyrannical then the Home was a vassal state and the children the silent serfs. Even matrons and masters were mere servants to the power of the management committees. But a good committee could find ways of humanising the Homes, scrounge money for holidays, ease regulations. Money was always short and even the best Home was poorer and stricter than any modern child would countenance. Clothes were patched, turned, cannibalised to make into new garments, accepted from neighbours or bought in anonymous bulk. Food was plain. Visitors were exceptional.

The shock of entering the strange new world of a Home was often overwhelming. Some children, moving from foster home or passing directly into care would be met with kindness and dog cart at the station. A warm meal and a smiling matron waited at the big house to welcome them. Others met a very different initiation into their new world. First they might be moved to a reception home where a stern-faced nurse bustled them into their first-ever and much dreaded bath, new, harsh clothes were substituted for their own, their hair was shorn and plain, unfamiliar food slammed down in front of them with the threat of a smack if they did not eat it all up. Then on they would travel to their new Home, alone in a train shut in the guard's van (in some cases) with a label attached. When they arrived they might wait for what seemed like hours in the emptiness and grandeur of a vast reception room until Matron, her hat perched perilously on her head, came to read the stringent rules of her establishment. And then came the unnerving plunge into the Home to meet the curious, seemingly antagonistic inmates, the jarring bells, the organised rushing to meals or household tasks.

Right: The children of the slums. No shoes or boots, assorted and patched clothes. This unusual picture tells it as it was. Few would have wandered far from the street of their birth. To them rumours of the homes must have been like news from the moon.
(Imperial War Museum)

Little wonder that the newcomer wet his bed night after night—great pity that he was soundly thrashed for it, even made to sit with his wet sheet over his head for shame or stand in his wet nightshirt in the cold corridor for all to see.

Most cruel was the separation of brother and sister. 'In our case,' one old girl remembers, 'my little brother aged three and myself about five were parted and sent as far away from each other as possible. Not only did this cause terrible upset to two small children but it severed us for ever as brother and sister. Also my poor mother (newly widowed with four babies under seven years of age) was unable to visit us very often. I was sent to Beckenham and my brother was sent to Norfolk. We were 14 and 17 when we met again. This sort of tragedy should be avoided, especially by the Church.'

One clergyman sought to alleviate the distress by taking scores of photographs of the children in each Home and carrying them from Home to Home so that brothers and sisters could at least see what each other looked like.

The logic of single sex Homes defies the modern mind. Even the founder of the Waifs and Strays at first wanted mixed homes, but the sexual obsessions of Victorian and Edwardian society made such an idea unstomachable. It was not until the thirties that staff started challenging the idea of single sex Homes and not until after the last war that they came into being.

During the twenties and thirties things got better for the Homes, though improvement was patchy and regional—even after the last war Homes could still be found where silence was enforced during meals and the children ate out of enamel bowls.

The loyalty of children to their Homes, however strictly run, is one of the recurring themes in any story of child care. It is not surprising. For a child who has lost everything, that which he calls home and she whom he calls matron are his sole anchors in a frightening world. An old boy who had no one recalls: 'A very sad thing happened to us boys. Mr. Pink and his wife left the Home to go to Canada to captain a ship on the lakes (he was ex-navy). We stood at the gate and watched his taxi go out of the road and I think we were all choked, everyone liked them both. Another master and matron came to take over but it wasn't the same.'

A young man returns from Canada to see the Home of his youth; he stands by the gate looking in at the unknown children playing in the garden. A smiling house parent walks up to speak to him, politely interested that he had once lived in the Home. But to the young man the house parent was new, he was not *his* 'uncle' and the children playing were not *his* children. Sadly he turns away, forced to realise that his Home days are ended, there is no going back, he must make a new beginning.

Where did they go, these children of the Homes, when the time came for them to leave? For the girls before the last war it was mainly to service in the great, and the lesser, homes of the aristocracy and gentry—'tween maids, kitchen maids, ladies' maids, they moved from the world of the Homes to the world below stairs. The local clergyman was bound to come round to the Home to pick himself a suitable girl to keep his house, he had first choice of the bunch. Other girls went to factories, as trained

Right: Clergy hurry to the refreshment tent after dedicating the beginnings of a new Home to the Almighty. A troop of scouts form a guard of honour. In those days (1913) Home children were segregated in their own scout troops (left facing: The foundation stone).

Below: St Chad's Home, Leeds (1937): The great sweep of the drive, the forbidding exterior—what a shock to a child fresh from the slums.

Left: A band of Fareham ladies, possibly led by Lady Larcom wife of Sir Thomas, first baronet of Heathfield, Fareham, opened the Industrial Home in 1878 to train laundry girls. By 1884 it was on its last legs and the Society took it over. By 1906 the old Home, shown left, was beyond repair and a new one was built on the site. The Home, now called St. Edith's was finally closed in 1968 when the master and matron and some of the children moved to Lancashire—over 100 miles away. Others were boarded out locally. In 1927 there were 30 girls between 14 and 16 in residence 'and subscribers and others can have servants from the Home which is chiefly self-supporting'. During the last war the children were evacuated first to Exeter where they were bombed out (no casualties), then to Sampford Peverell, and finally to Torquay. They moved back after the war—by now the 'laundry image' was dead, and in the early 1950s it became a mixed sex family Home of 24 children.

Right: Laundry girls at Fareham in 1890.

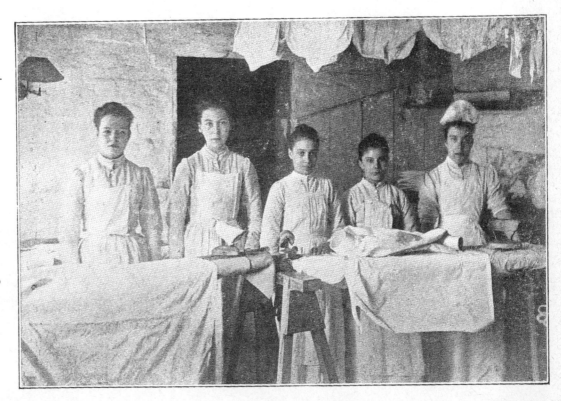

seamstresses many would find work in the rag trade, some became nursery nurses, fewer became nurses and a smattering, those with aptitude, good luck and powerful backing from their matron and the management committee made it to the professions, particularly teaching.

Many married and lived happily ever after. 'It was a wonder we grew up normal,' chuckled one old girl. But grow up normal many, very many of them did, and that must weigh heavily in any assessment of a hundred years of child care.

What happened to the boys? Some would be farm labourers, and amongst those who went abroad some would end up with their own small holdings. One Englishman eventually got himself a farm in the heart of Welsh-speaking Wales, and when he died locals packed the chapel where he was buried, a tribute to the quality of the man and the nature of his upbringing, who had started with all the cards stacked against him. Others became printers, factory workers, artisans, some did well in business—one did so well he left around a million pounds to the Children's Society—and at the other end of the scale there were those who went into service. They could mend their socks as easily as mend a threshing machine and were well equipped for work, but of the world outside the Home they knew precious little.

15

Left: 1930s Home girls. 'The matron has a motto, Aim High and she always said we were the smartest girls in Lowestoft. I can remember staff sitting up all night making summer dresses in boxed patterned material so that we should all look alike and be smart. What money the committee could not allow her for she gave out of her own pocket.'

Below: Standon Farm training school, around 1890. Again the uniform clothes—but coarse material and each boy with his hair cropped to a military shortness.

Right: A new arrival in the inter-war years.

Below: 1902, a young woman about to leave the Home for a life of service.

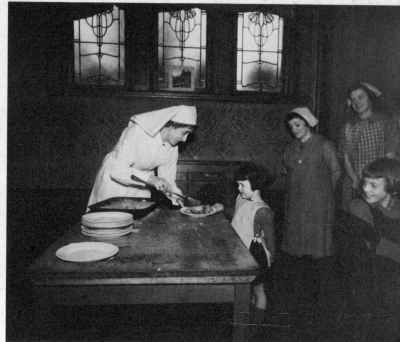

Over the years the food got steadily better—but even that varied wildly from Home to Home (above right). Before the last war 'The food was wholesome and nourishing. Lots of fish and meat. Porridge in the mornings and plenty of eggs. Cake for tea on Sundays.'

Above left: Self sufficiency—even for the boys. Three children show their prowess at sewing (1947).

Right: Boys in their natural state swimming in the Thames at Deptford while boys from a Home look enviously on.

April 1899
Ethel May Thompson.
'Dear Mrs. Brandreth,
Annie B who has been with me for six years is
most likely to take the situation as a cook in
my son's household. Ada R, now with us for
two and a half years will take Annie's place
here as a kitchen maid, and I would be very
happy if you could give me another of your
girls to take her place as a scullerymaid. All
your girls are most excellent and in every way
satisfactory, and they seem content with us.'

Queen Mary visiting a nursery. The Queen always retained a special affection for the Children's Society, knitting scarves for the children on the express understanding that it should not be given out that they were her work lest they were kept as mementos rather than worn.

At one with the children

For years everybody seemed involved with the future of the children in care—Royalty, the local villagers, clergy and bishops, school kids, businessmen, the aristocracy, even domestic pets and fairies were brought into the picture—everybody, that is, except the children themselves. They were a people apart to be loved, guided, prepared for the future but not consulted. While gala performances involving the cream of society raised money for them, they continued their daily tasks largely unaffected by the fuss that was going on around them.

If little children should be seen but not heard, it must have seemed to some of those early waifs and strays that they were meant neither to be seen nor heard. Partly this was a result of an enlightened policy not to use the children themselves as fund raisers lest this should appear to be exploiting them. But the result has been that it has taken until the last decade and even now only in part, to break down the massive reluctance of adults to listen to the children they are seeking to support and bring up. And there is a curious and partly substantiated fear that if the children begin to say loudly and clearly what they want from the carers and supporters, the old guard of voluntary helpers, fund raisers, supporters and VIPs will be tempted to back off. To use an old saying: there is a belief that if the children turn and bite the hand that feeds them, that hand will be withdrawn.

One helper recalls: 'When I commenced (in 1919) the more economically a society was run the more worthy of support. Then it was found that the stature of the children brought up in Homes was much lower than other children and more nourishing food was given, better food, clothing adapted to the seasons and holidays brought a higher standard. But of course, this meant a much higher expenditure until I felt we were giving our children more than the folk we were asking to support us could give theirs—then 1939 came and rationing righted this.'

The question to what extent it is proper to listen and act on the child's view of being in care is now one of the major issues for both the voluntary and statutory child care services. Can they be treated as truly part of the larger community with its freedoms, even its excesses, without losing the financial support and encouragement of that community? When the children were firmly behind four walls, issuing forth in carefully controlled groups on compulsory walks, bowing to the gentry (a thing some still recall with great anger) and offering a polite word when they were spoken to, they were objects of compassion. But in the present developing atmosphere of child care they are more likely to be pulling up your prize flowers from your garden as part of a treasure hunt, yelling in the streets after a disco or protesting vehemently that they are not given enough pocket money to buy cigarettes. A child has probably always wanted to know why he came into care and what was going to happen to him, now he is beginning to insist that he is told, that he sits in on the six-monthly reviews of his case and that he is involved in the planning of his future.

Inevitably the Children's Society has itself been a child of its time. It has reflected the values and assumptions of the society it sprang from and to which it had to appeal for support. There were exceptions however, even in the earliest days; Homes

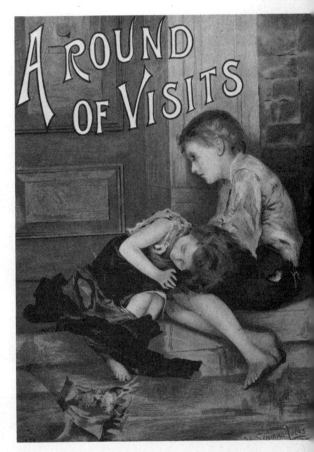

Money raising is the life blood of the voluntary societies. Publicity and the public's reaction to their work is all important. Children are powerful evokers of the charitable response and the sight of two pathetic waifs huddled on a doorstep was irresistible. Later children depicted nursery rhymes or Christmas carols, happy or sad, playing or pining, all were grist to the publicity drive to raise staggering sums of money to sustain the work—currently running at around £9 million a year for the Children's Society.

Queen Mary hesitantly receives a purse
from a member of the Pets League towards
the Society's funds. Pets were enrolled by their
owners who contributed on their behalf. The
late-lamented racehorse Arkle was just one of
a long line of distinguished animal members.

For many years a sale of work was organised by the Countess of Strathmore at the Dorchester Hotel to raise funds. Queen Elizabeth, now the Queen Mother, would attend and is here pictured meeting a crippled boy. Royalty and aristocracy featured large both in public meetings of the Society and in the behind the scenes activities. It was one of the unwritten 'jobs' of the upper class to be concerned with those at the bottom of the pile and they formed, and still form, a significant component in voluntary work.

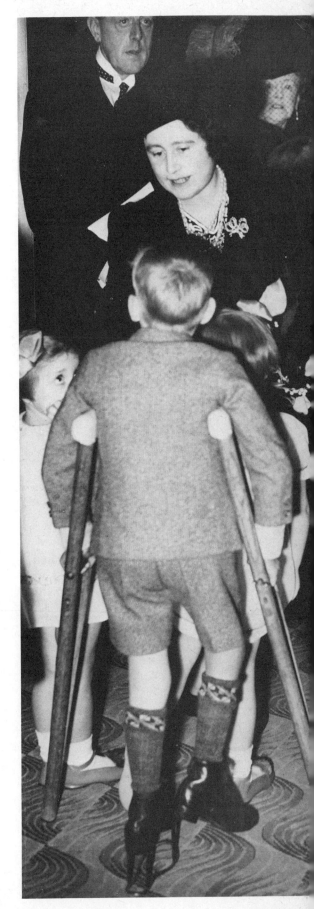

that did not insist on uniforms, that let the children mix with the local villagers, that listened to the children's needs and, gradually, over the years, these exceptions became more and more frequent. Children were no longer hurried back from school in silent lines, when a child won a scholarship to a grammar school she no longer had the anguish of having to turn it down, children were allowed home to their parents or relatives or to stay out with friends. They wore their own clothes and became indistinguishable from the rest of the community. They were given back their names and no longer referred to as numbers and in the fullness of time their Homes, distinguished as St. this or St. that were uncanonised, to become simply number 55 Beach Row, indistinguishable from number 53 or number 57.

One figure who for long stood out as a distinguishing mark of the Children's Society was the local clergyman. He it was who along with the doctor, the Poor Law guardian or the parents themselves, may have referred a child to the Society in the first place. It was to him that the Society appealed for foster parents, an appeal he passed on to his flock with all the authority of his pulpit. Whether or not the local children's Home was seen as part of the community or was isolated behind its walls, by and large ignored by the churchgoers could be affected by him. In return he got a regular and demure congregation of children from the Home to fill his emptying pews.

As time passed, church going became no longer compulsory for older children. The Society altered its rules so that christians who were not avid churchgoers would still be eligible as staff or fosterparents. Even the post of chaplain to the local Home, invariably filled by the local vicar, was dropped so that staff and children could worship where they felt most at home.

Now a new champion of the children has emerged—the social worker. Recently long-haired social workers have been seen physically battling with the authorities who want to close down Homes against the children's wishes and there is talk of children going on strike. Real integration is in the air. Family centres to which children and their parents can come during the day are springing up as Homes close down. Staff, no longer protected by their uniform now do not even have the security of a Home in which they can impose the rules, like the children and their parents they too are exposed to the ebb and flow of local politics and opinion.

Such changes are disturbing and many have wondered whether a huge voluntary organisation such as the Children's Society can survive such changes. But it has changed many times in a hundred years and still its vast army of voluntary helpers remain loyal. They turn out in all weathers, often when it seems madness to do so, to rattle their collecting boxes, organise fêtes, run charity shops, seek sponsorship to keep the show on the road. For years groups of children could be found busily stitching away while an adult read to them, making clothes for the 'waifs and strays'. In 1889 one such group developed into the Children's Union—an organisation for kids up to 16 who clubbed together to raise cash to sponsor beds for the hundreds of cripples who were pouring into care. It became a common sight in the Society's specialist Homes to see a huge brass plaque secured to the end of a cot proudly inscribed with the name of the sponsoring branch of the CU. Who were these strange benefactors called 'Dulwich' or

Above: Flowers for the patroness—a timeless ceremony which has been carried out by each generation of little girls.

Top right: Princess Alice, Duchess of Gloucester became patron of the Children's Union in 1936. She has continued her active support for the work of the Society ever since.

Below: Each new home began with the ceremonial laying of the foundation stone by a local figure. Here His Grace the Duke of Northumberland lays the stone at St. Aiden's Boys' Home, Tynemouth, now a family home.

Generations of stars of stage and screen have always given generously of their time and talents to support charities. Pop stars have continued the tradition. Here, children from Hambro House, Roehampton, paint Easter eggs with the Beatles.

Right: Until the last war loosened up the rules children would only venture out of the homes in twos and under escort. Integration with the local community was not encouraged.

Below: Pound Day, when the villagers brought a pound or more of often much needed sustenance to the local children's Home has been an annual event for nearly a century. Sometimes the food was passed on to even more needy families: 'It was usually in May and my mother used the ingredients to make one big cake which was a combined birthday cake for all six of us children. She could only do this on Pound Day.'

Masques and pageants were extremely popular as a way of raising money throughout the first forty years of the century. School children, voluntary helpers and their families would be involved, but the waifs and strays stayed in their Homes, getting on with the hard task of preparing themselves for a largely inhospitable world. Pictured left is a Cambridge pageant just before the last war.

'Frodsham' the anonymous occupants of the cots must have speculated—perhaps the same way as Third World children must nowadays wonder who are their foreign benefactors who have 'adopted' them through one of the charities now specialising this kind of aid.

The two worlds co-existed but rarely co-joined. Sometimes the world of the voluntary fund raisers would infringe on the consciousness of the children in care when a fête was held in the Home's grounds or on Pound Day when open day was kept in the local homes and the community, after bringing its gifts was free to wander around and meet the inmates (a term used for the children up to the last war).

A village child recalls the monastic seclusion of one Home in the 1920s. 'My first memories are of them coming into the village church, clothed in long black coats and black hats, they wended their way to the darkest and coldest part of the church. They were allowed no contact with the village children. Education was given in the Home itself. But then came the great day when our schoolmaster told us the Home children were to come to the village school. I am afraid they lost our sympathy when we found that they were not all orphans. Perhaps this was a good thing as they were soon talked out of their shyness and we knew their case histories down to the last sordid detail.'

The idea that the Homes were full of orphans took a long time to die. Indeed even now school children will write, their hearts overflowing, to ask how they can help all the poor children who have neither fathers nor mothers. There is something cut and dried about the status of orphan which appeals in a way that the reality—children who have been neglected or abused, who are beyond control or in need of special care, whose parents are ill or incapable—does not appeal or is not readily understood.

The stigma of being a Home child was often counteracted by the masters or matrons who instilled in their charges a pride in their way of life. 'Don't take any notice of them, Johnny' Matron would say as the village kids threw insults as they passed, 'you are worth two of them any day.' It was a pride that was not entirely misplaced, for they were well trained, their manners were often much better than their contemporaries and through the interest the aristocracy took in them they were often exposed to a way of life they would never otherwise have learnt about. But what was it all for? As one matron said: 'We were bringing them up to have middle-class values, and they would never again feel at ease in their old environment, but they were not middle class. They were trained to work, mostly, as artisans and servants and many never got over the tensions between the class values instilled into them and their humble positions in society.'

Meal time at Standon Farm Training School.
The grim task of preparing the children for the
harsh realities of life left little time for holidays.
Discipline, silence during meals, work from
dawn to dusk, these were the remedial and
educational ingredients used to correct the
effects of slum life on the young inmates.

CHAPTER 3 Celebration

Children were in Homes to be brought up proper, not to have fun. That was the Victorian way of seeing things and its influence persisted into the twenties and thirties. But children, being contrary, enjoyed themselves in the cracks, so to speak, where the cement of the rules was broken. They bucked the system in a thousand ways. Each Home had a punishment book. They read like the official dispatches from the running battle against the children's high spirits. 1932, August 21, Bournemouth, the entry for one week runs: 'Impertinence; failing to show respect after previously being warned; breaking line on way to church; throwing dirt at each other; throwing mugs about and causing monitor much trouble; being concerned in taking another boy's writing things on to playground and leaving them there; carelessly losing cap; knocking small boy about; stealing apples from orchard and lying.'

'If we were caught doing anything it was bed every day at 4 pm for a fortnight,' one crippled girl recalls of her Home forty years ago. 'In those days it was an absolute sin to walk on the grass, so we used to do it out of devilment. You can bet your life there was someone watching from the windows. The window would go up, Matron would clap her hands and you would have to report to her when you got inside. All treats would be stopped. If we were on punishment we would take a ball up onto the roof and play in our nighties while everyone was having tea. If we got caught that was double punishment—a month of 4 pm bed!'

Scrumping apples: that was the great offence and the greatest pleasure. 'One day when I was up a tree filling my knickers with apples,' another girl recalls, 'I saw a glimpse of the gardener behind the wall where he had been watching me. I almost fell down the tree. He got hold of me by the scruff of my neck and took me to Matron. While he was telling Matron I was standing outside and the other girls were standing at the end of the corridor. I got hold of the apples and rolled them down the corridor to the others so Matron wouldn't find them on me. Do you know she never searched me, just sent me to bed without any tea—to think I could have eaten all those apples!'

One children's Home, perhaps others too, realised breaking rules was part of any holiday and declared a two-day moratorium on house rules over Christmas. 'Our greatest thrill was running up and down the carpeted front staircase which we weren't allowed to use all year.' The Home made up for its latitude on Good Friday when absolute silence prevailed all day.

Before the twenties holidays were Holy-days. Sunday was a day of great seriousness tempered with country walks. Religion was all too popular with the staff of children's Homes and was ladled out like the Virol cook supplied to the lines of waiting children outside the kitchen. Those were the days before a healthy scepticism had had its astringent effect on the established church. Refusal to take your religious medicine led to a beating. The ability of children to develop their own faith in later years is yet more evidence of a child's awe-inspiring skill at overcoming the disadvantages adults put in its way.

Many failed: the rules and the institution were too strong for them. Those were the children who would grow up never feeling happy unless surrounded by the

Ragged children drinking from a fountain in London in 1913. This picture was first used in an appeal for money to send Homes' children on holiday in 1921. 'Young England of the slums on holiday. Is it good enough?' read the caption. Depicting a state of affairs before the Great War clearly it was not.

noise and bustle of others, the shallow relationships of the big group, the comfort of a framework of external rules. They would go on to be the pillars of many a local church.

Others, those strong enough to rebel but not able to see any good wrapped up in the bad, never got over the compulsory learning of collects every Sunday, the interrogations over the sermon or the daily religious readings. They were as lost to the real message the Society was set up to proclaim as if they had been left on the streets. Vicars now complain that they can no longer count on their pews being filled with Home children. For the children it is better that they can now make up their own minds.

For all that, church provided a break. In almost all Homes at first no one left the Home grounds except to go to school or to church—or for a supervised walk. But no one could put a boundary on imagination, and for those with eyes to see and the will to act, the walk to church provided split second opportunities to assess the qualities of the village boys or girls, hint or wink at assignations and the material for endless fantasies of romance and adventure. Children did run away from the Homes, they did climb over the walls, play truant, slip out after dark.

Alas, those were seen not as heroes by the staff but as disturbing influences. 'Why do you always tell me to stop doing things?' a child asks its harassed parent. When a child is in care the question needs to be asked more often, but until recently has been hardly asked at all.

But there were real holidays as well. At first it was only an occasional treat as no money was made available for a holiday. Easter Monday meant a visit to the pictures at one Home. 'I used to live on that happy memory for weeks afterwards. We had sandwiches and a cake each at a cafe before the show. I used to describe my cake in detail to my friends that had not been.' Another boy remembers being totally perplexed at the annual visit to the pantomime. The whole idea of a play, actors feigning reality or a story depicted on stage was foreign to him.

Below: Children and staff from St. Saviour's, Shrewsbury on holiday at New Brighton, August 1939.

Dressed up in pearls for May Day. May Day and Whitsun were amongst the few occasions when the Home children joined in the general fun.

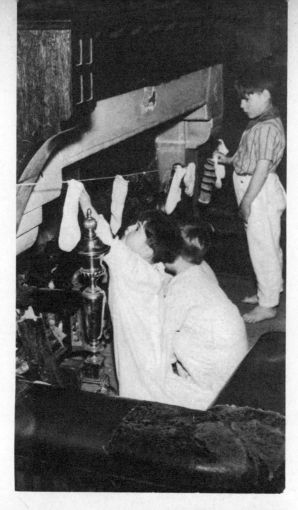

Christmas was always the great celebration. '1946, Christmas stockings, sweets, toys, books! Turkeys and geese, chickens, puddings, cakes and jellies galore! Parcels from "Uncles" and "Aunts", Christmas trees, parties, treats. There are coins for the Christmas puddings, there are crackers and decorations. Friends of the children gave of their best and came to see the children enjoy themselves, and themselves felt better and happier for it,' wrote an enthusiastic supporter. Thirty-one years before that an old boy wrote, somewhat obscurely, from Quebec: 'I can remember a Christmas I spent twelve years ago in England begging a crust of bread, but the Waifs and Strays Society came to my rescue and gave me not only bread but every comfort I could desire (although I did not think so at the time), perhaps I do now.'

Children could play in the playroom (far left) or in the grounds of the Home (near left) as these girls are doing at Ashbourne, but the world outside the Homes was largely denied to them. Note the girls all wearing the same clothes. At least the early habit of cropping the children's hair had ended. The girls look pretty and happy enough despite their uniformity.

But treats could be jeopardised by well-meaning adults. One wonders, for instance, just how unanimous was the agreement of the crippled girls at St. Chads Home in Leeds in the First World War when, after making 13,361 pairs of socks for the brave lads out in the trenches they 'unanimously agreed that all money given them for treats should be spent on more socks for the soldiers, and H.M. the Queen graciously acknowledged the gift.'

By the 1930s holidays were becoming more frequent—although there was still precious little money about. Clothes, food, bedding would be crammed into tea chests, a lorry or cart commandeered from local wellwishers and the Home would move out as one man to the nearest railhead. Everyone went on holiday together. There was no going home to mother, even if she was willing and able to take her child. The family of the Home sank or swam together so one never felt out of it. Empty schoolhouses, village halls, rectories, homes lent by friends, a swap with another Home, or a farmer's field would be the destination.

'We went to camp one summer. I don't know where it was, I've often wondered. There was not a building in sight anywhere except the farm where we all filled our palliasses with straw. I never put enough in mine—I can still feel the ache.

'We had to sleep in bell tents with our feet to the pole and nothing touching the canvas walls. The master used to come round after we were all tucked in, with a mallet and make sure the pegs were in securely. Any kit bags touching the canvas he knocked away with the mallet. One kit bag was a boy's head, in my tent. He only copped it once.

'We got our water for washing from a pond in the corner of a field where the cows drank. You couldn't reach the water without going through thick sloshy mud. The water had green slime on it. I still hate water.'

The last war changed all this, as it changed so many things for children in care. Now holidays with relatives or friends are frequent. One well-wisher recently organised to take a party of boys to an empty school house in Spain, others go hiking, mountaineering, canoeing. During school holidays the Homes are alive with comings and goings. It is difficult to realise it is the same society that eighty years ago only allowed one day's holiday a year.

This picture, an imaginative leap forward by the artist Margaret Tarrant from her more famous picture 'All things bright and beautiful' in which the Christ child is surrounded by children, angels and animals, hung for years at the Children's Society's crippled boys home at Pyrford. The Home was taken over by the NHS and rechristened the Rowley Bristow Hospital in 1950. The artist has captured the feeling that the handicapped are particularly loved by Christ, a feeling behind much of the philanthropic work with cripples in the first thirty years of the century. A copy of this picture was sent, in 1929, as a Christmas gift to Princess Elizabeth. The Duchess of York accepted the gift on the young princess's behalf and her lady in waiting wrote: 'Will you please tell the children at Pyrford how much the Duchess appreciates the picture, and she feels sure her little daughter will as she grows older and sees it often.'

Courage and hope

'I don't really believe there is a God up there somewhere, but if my Aunt was here she would be quite upset.' Anna was making a recording for the 1981 International Year of the Disabled Person. She was trying to get across just what it is really like to be stuck in a wheelchair for hours on end suffering from spina bifida. Her Cypriot parents had brought her to England where she was staying in a specialist Home because equivalent treatment was not available in her country. Why didn't she believe in God?

'Well, there's all sorts of bad things going on in the world. I mean if there was a God why doesn't God stop them? I mean he's meant to love people not let other people carry on killing. Anyway, why am I disabled? What have I done against God—I mean why does he have to pick on me, can't he pick on somebody his own size? OK, maybe I've insulted him now, but I didn't insult him then did I, sixteen years ago. I haven't done anything against him so why throw it at me? Why throw it at most disabled people, why make them suffer for something that somebody else has done?'

There is a quality, hard to define, powerful in its impact which seems the peculiar prerogative of the suffering child, though Anna—or any other handicapped or suffering young person—would not thank an observer for saying so. The main concern is to get as much done with what remaining limb or part of brain still functions as is humanly possible. A handicapped child with use of neither arms or legs will roll himself out of bed in the morning, shuffle, push and worm his way into his clothes, bump his way to the top of the stairs and give his incredulous houseparent the shock of his life. The courage and hope the child shows calls for its own deep response from those who look after him. It is a response that may need time to mature, but many who have worked with handicapped children would now do nothing else.

Anna.

'I love every minute of it here,' said a one time market gardener now working with handicapped children. 'When I am with these children they are normal children to me. They are dearly loved.' The work in the small Leicestershire residential nursery for disabled children had captured her heart. A child had recently died and the staff were moved by his death. He had been with them for just over five years, a grossly handicapped spastic child, mentally and physically retarded but a child who loved to be nursed, caressed, spoken to. When it became clear he was going to die he had not been sent away to hospital but had stayed with the 'family' who knew and loved him. He died in the early hours of a spring morning in the arms of the matron who cared so deeply for him.

There are fourteen children from babies up to seven years old in that Home. They are a lot of work. In one year those fourteen get through 22,000 clean nappies, 9,000 feeders and 38,325 gallons of bath water. The staff sew 1,120 name tapes into their clothes and clean 9,350 shoes during the year. But when a boy like Jason, severely handicapped, rolls out of bed and crawls along the corridor to tap quietly at matron's door for an early morning cuddle, the statistics of handicap melt before the human reality.

The Children's Society can lay fair claim to be amongst the pioneers of work with these children. Cripples' Homes opened in the last century and by the 1930s the

This is Elinor at St. Nicholas, Pyrford. From
the first she was "very quiet and serious". But
as she grew stronger: "the faintest flicker of a
smile could be seen on her fair gentle face"
*(Brothers and Sisters Quarterly Magazine
1895)*

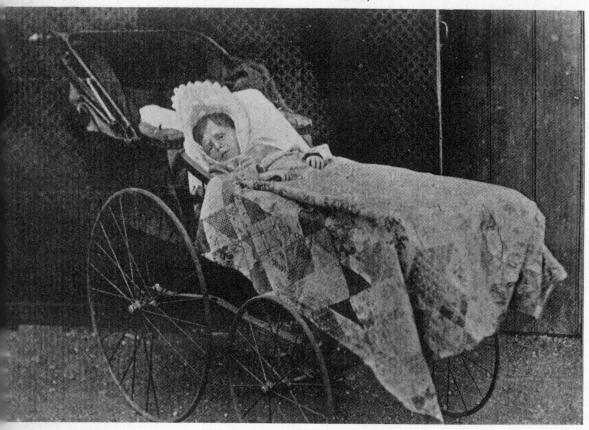

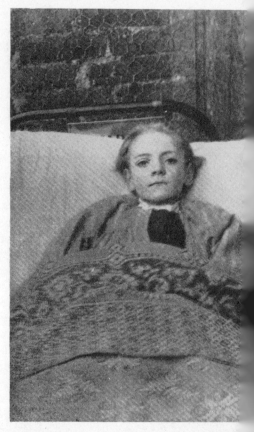

Lizzie lay on her back for 3 years 3 months
St. Nicholas, Pyrford, before she died
peacefully. Edward Rudolf described her a
"bright and cheerful that she was beloved b
all who knew her . . . When asked how she
was, she invariably replied, 'Nicely thank
you!'"

Courage and hope spring from a child's trust and an adult's love. Here one of the staff at the Leicestershire residential nursery feeds a handicapped child who will never be able to feed himself.

A line of cripples wend their way back from an outing. Note the uniform clothes and capes, the leg-irons and, of course, the single file so loved by the Home staff.
(*Imperial War Museum*)

Society had not only convalescent Homes for those with weak hearts, but a fully equipped orthopaedic hospital. It seems to have been the first to introduce water therapy. In 1931 the Pyrford children, some who had not moved from their chairs or frames under their own steam for years, swam for the first time in their custom-built swimming pool. For the able bodied it must be impossible to imagine what that freedom felt like, as fear gave way to wonder and limbs useless on dry land began to work under the buoyant effect of the water.

The breakthroughs in treatment continued and quickened. At the Halliwick School in North London where Anna has lived for ten years, fifteen-year-old Stacey now 'talks' to staff through her Bliss board. Unable to speak or control her muscles enough to write, she can, with great effort, point to the symbols on the large board in front of her which is her link with the moving, noisy world about her. 'I would like to be able to walk and talk. I would like to be like my sister Nicole. Not being able to walk is cruel. People who can walk are lucky. I would like to be able to eat on my own'; Stacey laboriously spelt out the phrases.

Two levers operate her electric wheelchair. Her flailing arms strike them in succession forcing the chair to obey her will. Countless times the chair smashes against the corridor walls as the wheels manoeuvre erratically. She is happy but one thing upsets her. Unable to explain, she has fought the chair into the passage and is now tossing her arms at the ceiling where a black fire bell stares down at her. It is the harsh note of the bell she hates. Slowly her companion discovers her love of music, learns about the record player she has at home (for she only attends the school during the day) and watches as she spells out her favourite tune *Bright Eyes*, The theme music from *Watership Down*, the tale of how a small band of rabbits, through pluck and luck win a place for themselves in the sun.

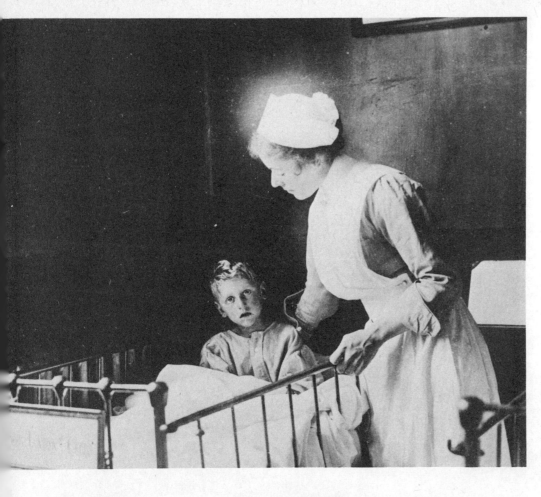

A very sick boy being nursed in his cot before the First World War. The name of the sponsors of the cot hangs at his feet but is not clearly discernible.
(Imperial War Museum)

It is that place in the sun for which the handicapped and their helpers have struggled for nearly a century. Technology, medical care and love are giving substance to the Christmas hope of Handel's *Messiah*: 'Then shall the eyes of the blind be opened, and the ears of the deaf unstopped, then shall the lame man leap as an hart, and the tongue of the dumb shall sing.'

'I got TB hip when I was eighteen months old. My mother left me when I was taken ill and I never saw her again', recalls an old Halliwick girl looking back fifty years. Those were the days when TB was the scourge. Children born with the sort of physical handicaps now being helped would have died long before they could have received treatment—even if suitable treatment was available, which it wasn't. TB is now largely defeated, but then it needed the most particular care and the outcome was always uncertain.

'I spent four and a half years flat out on a frame, all day and every day. Sometimes I would be lying with my head down and my feet in the air to improve my circulation. We even had school lessons when I was on the frame, reading and writing.' She took her first, faltering steps when she was six. 'I think it was through neglect that I had this hip in the first place. I don't think it was "from above" as they say. I can't see any good having come from me being like this—but you can't go through life being bitter, it's not worth it.'

Although life saving, a childhood spent suspended, often at acute angles from a great wooden frame must have been immensely frustrating to children eager for action. Another girl remembers arriving, at the age of four, at a Home in the North. 'As soon as I arrived the Matron and a nurse took hold of my hands and put them on a pole hanging from the ceiling and stretched my whole limbs and then put me in a spinal carriage and strapped me from head to foot where I stayed for two years being too weak

The children roasting in the sun were suffering from TB and were kept totally still to arrest the progress of the disease. The sun was believed to have a curative effect and each child has a sun blind to protect his face. At night they slept in a hut swaddled in warm clothes, to make sure they got as much fresh air as possible. 'The other day I was taking some visitors round the Home (writes a correspondent) and the children were so brown they would not believe they were English until I showed them the soles of their feet.'

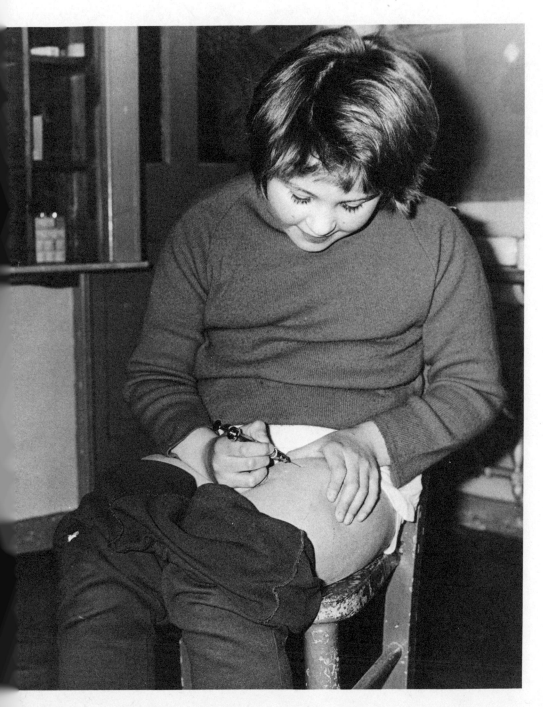

By the 1960s the Children's Society had three Homes for diabetic children from difficult home backgrounds. They were taught to control their diet and administer their own insulin.

A sub-prefect at Halliwick school learns to type in the fifties. The students have always been prepared for work, but not always for life outside. The battle to 'liberate' the regime of the ordinary children's Homes, allowing the children greater freedom and responsibility, is only now being joined for the handicapped child. Until 1978 there was a rule at Halliwick that no child was able to go round one side of the Home because he would then be out of sight of a staff member. To treat a handicapped child as an independent person is one of the hardest lessons staff have to learn.

for a plaster of paris cast. I can remember my mother screaming when they put me o: the pole. One day I decided to feel for the straps and to unfasten the top one so that could move my head a little further round, but my nurse didn't like that so I promise not to do it again.'

The other great cure for TB was sunlight and fresh air. Children would spen all day baking under the hot sun and at night, even in London, they would spend man a summer evening sleeping on the balcony. 'A sheepdog, Rover, would stay out with u to make sure we came to no harm.'

Handicapped the children were, but that did not stop them working—an playing. As with their counterparts in the 'normal' Homes before the last war the childre all had duties to do, sweeping, laying the tables, tidying the bedrooms, although their dutie were not so onerous as those of their able limbed brothers and sisters. 'One girl who had beautiful artificial leg used to stand it in a corner of the room while she used the broo: to support her as she swept.' There would be needlework for the older girls and the would do all the Home's mending. 'Some mornings two of the nurses would take a par of children out in the donkey cart. One nurse would drive and the other ride on the ste at the back. If the donkey wanted to stop the nurse at the back ran round ar encouraged him with slaps and shouts. Then he would decide to race and she had jump back on the step very quickly. Sometimes we had picnics in the woods and v even took the spinal carriages with their occupants to these.'

For some, TB struck later, after they had left the Homes. For all the fresh a and food they had while in care many had been fundamentally damaged by t wretched conditions of their birth and earliest years. Even now poverty exacts a hi price in increased mortality and in the hungry, cold and damp lives of the poor of t early part of the century death struck with a frequency which would have made t middle classes shudder.

Sarah was just one of those many waifs who could not escape the ill effect of their earliest years. She was in service and well liked. The cold she had developed during the winter months did not clear up and she went to see the doctor. The doctor sat very still after he had examined her and did not speak. He told her she must go to hospital if she wished to get well as she was suffering from TB. He did not say that she had galloping consumption and had less than six months to live. Her employer went to visit her in hospital and a visitor from the Children's Society called regularly. Her family lived in the depressed North and her mother had already died of TB. The visitor recalls: 'She was a very sweet girl and most brave and patient through her trial. I don't think she knew how serious her case was until the last six weeks. Then the complaint was going down to her tummy and she was suffering from bed sores. The last time I saw her she would not let me call a nurse as "the nurses are all very busy, they have a lot to do". It was Wednesday and I said that I would be down again at the weekend but I saw by her look that she knew she would not be here. I said how very sorry I was that she had had such a hard time. She made a strange reply: "I like it that way". Only once have I had a glimpse of what she tried to convey and I cannot quite recapture it. I think she thought that she would be all right in our Father's Kingdom of loving kindness if she bore this great cross gallantly. It was very affecting. She seemed to gain a quiet dignity in her suffering far beyond her nineteen years.'

Stacey talking to her mother, using Bliss symbols.

Homesteading near Lloydminster, Alberta. 'In the spring of 1921 we headed for Prince Albert,' wrote one old Home boy, 'and from there to Eldred, Saskatchewan, where we too up homesteads. I bought a team of oxen, buil a log cabin and broke my first land. We bough violins which we learnt to play, and we began playing for dances in the schools.'
(E. Brown Collection, Provincial Archives of Alberta.)

Exodus

'It seems I was born in London, but my earliest recollections are of the Isle of Wight. When my grandmother died—it must have been late in 1905—I found myself being taken across to the mainland in January 1906 to the village of Otterbourne, Hampshire. There I was placed in the care of an elderly widow, Eliza Hoskins, whose address was Belmont cottages. I lived with Mrs Hoskins for six years.

'From Belmont cottages I was taken to St. Aldelm's Home for boys at Frome, Somerset. There were about forty-eight boys in the Home and I enjoyed being with the others but discipline was strict and the food scanty.

'In the spring of 1913, someone asked: "Who would like to go to Canada?" I grasped the opportunity. Just a few of us were taken to Liverpool by the superintendent who showed us more affection than at any other time. I was fourteen years old and weighed all of eighty pounds. On May 16 about twenty-five of us sailed on the Tunisian.'

Over 100,000 children moved to Canada between 1870 and 1930, the period of the main emigration, and yet others were sent to Australia, New Zealand, Southern Rhodesia and South Africa. To the authorities responsible for them they were escaping from the unemployment, slums and vice which always threatened to suck them back. Some children must have had mixed feelings about their salvation.

'There's no beer nearer than Quebec, forty-five miles away,' wrote one Londoner from the dry wilderness of Canada. There they lived, ex-slum dwellers who might not have seen a cow before, in a land of wild horses, roaming cattle, wolves and home-spun clothes—and deep, deep snow. 'I always hated the snow,' wrote one girl who lost her feet through frost bite.

They had to be tough to survive the shock of emigration—and most of them were. Thomas Short, born in York came into care in February 1886. But he didn't get on in his first Home, the grim looking Standon Farm Training School, so he moved. Three months later he was moved again. 'We are sorry to have to report,' wrote his housemaster, 'that although the behaviour of the boys, on the whole, has been good, still there have been three attempts to run away. The first attempt was made by Thomas Short and William Harris, and was not very serious. The second time Thomas Short was again the offender and John Jones, an older boy, who is now removed to Standon. They were away two whole days and a night before they were finally captured at Bromborough by the police and brought back.'

'The third time Thomas Short took with him two smaller boys, but they were soon caught. T. Short was caned and severely reprimanded, but he came to Kingsley with the character of a runaway and, so far, seems inclined to keep it up.' Master Short was soon back at Standon and within three months—on the last day of May 1887, set sail for Canada, well equipped by nature for the hazards of life in the colonies.

Thirty-four years later things were still done in a rush. 'In May 1921 I was asked if I would like to go to Canada. After a few days of thinking it over I decided to make the big move. We left Liverpool on June 10 and landed in Quebec on June 19 and we were in Sherbrooke (the reception centre) the next day. After spending one week in Sherbrooke I was placed on a farm. In those days we put in long hours, from am to 8 and 9 pm.'

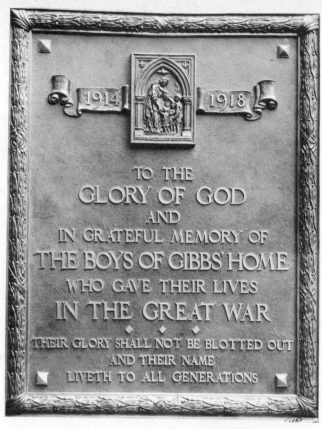

Left: 'The bronze tablet erected to the memory of the Old Boys from the Gibbs Home who died in the Great War was unveiled by Brigadier General Draper, DSO. It was especially appropriate that the General should perform the ceremony because he had under his command the 117th Battalion and the 5th Canadian Mounted Rifles which had the strongest representation from the Gibbs Home and sustained the highest casualties. The total casualties discovered up to date are 74 killed and 120 wounded.'—Sherbrooke Daily Record October 6 1921. The Society's crest, the Church receiving children to her care, stands at the top of the tablet. Over 80 boys who had emigrated to Sherbrooke in 1920 and 1921 attended the unveiling.

Below: Boys, staff and local dignitaries outside the Gibbs Home after the unveiling ceremony.

A party of children leaving London . . . and arriving at Fremantle, Australia. They had been shipped over by the Fairbridge Society which arranged passages for Home children and put them up in its farm schools in Australia. 'I remember,' recalls a master of a Home in Sevenoaks in the thirties, 'taking three boys up to London for emigration to Australia. One of the three had a brother, too young to go, but allowed to see him off. He was crying on the platform and a strange gentleman asked why and took his name. When we got back to Kent we had instructions to put the younger brother on the next boat— the stranger was none other than the High Commissioner for the Australian State to which they were emigrating.' Emigration of children to Australia stopped in 1957.

'It doesn't cost any more to feed a child than a chicken,' argued one of the farmers. 'We were the cheapest slave labour the farmers ever had,' said one of the boys.

The girls and boys were amazed at the new world—which they saw fleetingly before being plunged into their life of toil, 'I remember the red-coated soldiers coming up around the big house in the evenings and lying around in the grass. They were never allowed inside. The wee girls were allowed to talk to the soldiers but I don't think older girls were', an old girl recalls from the turn of the century.

Romance blossomed for one enterprising local. In the pre-dawn stillness of a summer night in 1895 he leaned a ladder against the wall of the girls' reception Home in Sherbrooke, shinned up it and (presumably by pre-arrangement with the young lady concerned) carried off 'the best wife in the world'. He then joined the Salvation Army.

The voyage from Liverpool to Canada seems for many to have been an ordeal of seasickness or boredom; for others, many of whom had never seen the sea or a boat before, the experience must have been mind-blowing. 'Most of the passengers were ill throughout the voyage,' recalls one boy. 'The little ones were very uncertain whether to look on Father Neptune as friend or foe,' recalls one of their guardians. 'They generally preferred to keep their eyes closed, rolled up in blue blankets on the deck looking, as one passenger remarked, like little rabbits in their burrows.' When the little rabbits eventually sneaked out they were greeted by 'The Rev. Fox, a missionary to the North American Indians who held a nice little service on board the *Numidian* for the children and gave them two interesting and instructive addresses.'

1913 was a good year for emigration. The Children's Society sent one hundred and eight boys to Canada who were 'provided with situations within a short time of arrival'. But matters did not rest there. It was commonplace for a child to be uprooted once, twice, and in some cases three or four times before they were suited. The farmer to whom they went might go through a bad patch and simply send back the boy he could no longer afford—or they might just not get on together (though the Home children seem to have been willing to put up with a lot before they complained).

Above: Learning to follow a plough. The training at Standon Farm Training School made the Home children welcome immigrants—especially when the Canadian authorities started to clamp down on the flow of young and ill-prepared children into the province.

Facing: June 1923. A White Star liner in Liverpool docks similar to the SS Canada on which twenty-four boys from the Society emigrated that month. One of the boys' masters went on board and reported: 'The boys are sharing four berth cabins with wire mattresses and there is abundant food and well cooked. In everything they were better provided for than I was though travelling second, in 1912.'
It was the second party of boys to go to Canada under the Society that year—but no girls had emigrated since the end of the War. Emigration for girls was to start again the following year for the 'Waifs and Strays'.
(*Merseyside Maritime Museum*)

POST OFFICE

'There are a large number of destitute and neglected children rescued by English philanthropic agencies from bad surroundings. This class would yield a considerable number of child-emigrants . . . it is clear that they should be sent as early as possible so that they may be more thoroughly acclimatised and accustomed to colonial life. Such a system however would not allow time for the discovery of any inherited taint.'— Edward de M. Rudolf, The Guardian, 21 May 1911.

'Off to Canada'.

"These Little Ones."

A letter has just been received from a young man who was cruelly deserted by his father and step-mother, but had seven years' training in a Home. He has been five years in Canada, is doing remarkably well, and is very happy, but still affectionately remembers his former days at the Home.

A girl, too, has been able to go out to an uncle in Australia, and assist in keeping an hotel.

Distances were vast and a boy being moved from the reception centre to the farm, or back to the reception centre travelled usually on his own in those early days, with a label on his jacket. 'We had tags on our coats like bags of potatoes.' Boys of fourteen might move, in exceptional cases, two hundred miles from one employer to another.

Those who had been trained at Standon Farm in England took well to their new life. One old boy recalls that as economic depression began to set in 'If you didn't come from Standon Farm you had little chance of getting work.' With the deepening depression came a reduction, and finally a halt, to emigration.

Clearing land, handling a plough, flailing wheat without hitting your ears and watching out for bears—it was a life almost unbelievably strange to us, strange enough to them, but one which left many ready to strike out on their own once their indentures were over.

At the age of eighteen some would go north to try their hand at mining, or even trapping, others west to the great wheat plains or to stake out a claim and break the virgin land, yet others would slip south across the border into the United States where wages were higher and there was no stigma attached to the Home boys.

Still others were themselves reaped in the bitter harvest of the First World War. Strong, young, with few attachments and used to an institutional life they were prime candidates for the forces and they flocked to the colours. In the ensuing carnage scores of them died.

56

A party of children from the Children's Society lines up for a group photograph aboard the White Star liner Doric before setting sail for Canada on Friday April 25 1930.

Children in a Home trying on their gas masks.

War

CHAPTER 6

Hannah was born two months after hostilities were declared. Her father joined the King's Own Scottish Borderers and was drafted to the front. Her mother, already weak, broke down under the enforced separation and Hannah was taken by a sympathetic clergyman to the Waifs and Strays. Then came the terrible Battle of Mons and her father was overcome with poison gas. As he lay dying his last recorded wish was for his daughters: 'Above everything make them good, and especially the baby'. The nurse who was attending him heard and arranged for Hannah to be boarded out with foster parents in Sussex. At Talbot House, a rest home at Poperinghe for men back from the salient, the army chaplain who had opened the home, the Rev. Tubby Clayton, took up her cause amongst the men as they came to rest, eat, pray and go up to Ypres to die.

'This little girl, whom none of us had ever seen, was the object of the most affectionate solicitude among small and great,' he wrote. 'The Military Police in the prison at Ypres collected eagerly on her behalf even during the exceedingly rough period of April, 1917.

'Major Harry Jago, D.S.O., M.C. of 2nd Devons asks anxiously for her in the last letter before his death. One Lancashire lad, than whom no more loyal friend could be met with, told me for three Sundays in succession how his officer was giving a prize for the best-kept mules. And it was not until one night, when he came in triumph and laid the prize money in my hand for the little girl, that I knew the secret of his ambition.'

The child grew to be tall and bright, affectionate and with a great love of all things beautiful. When adoption became possible in 1926 she was adopted by her foster parents. She did not know then, and probably still does not know, that they are not her real parents who were destroyed in that great and senseless war.

But there was no shortage of Volunteers for the slaughter. Even 'Tom Tit' a ten-year-old foster boy tried to enlist. The editor of the Waifs and Strays magazine wrote, in 1916: 'Our Role of Honour is a record of which we have cause to be proud—nine hundred old boys in the country's forces and some forty of them called on during the year to lay down their lives—six commissions gained for work well done—many masters of homes away on active duty—every eligible member of the "Home" office staff either serving or ready to serve when his call should come.'

'This on the one hand—on the other, an unceasing inflowing stream of "war cases", children of soldiers and sailors asking for care and a home. Of some six hundred applications none were refused.'

As the destruction continued so were orphans created by the hundred. 'I thank you very much for your kind wishes for me when I return to duty,' wrote one wounded old boy with whom, as with most of its children, the Society had tried to keep in touch. 'I consider God has dealt kindly with me up to the present, when I realise that I escaped so lightly.

'You see we commenced our engagement at two o'clock on the Monday afternoon with 750 men and although we carried the enemy's trenches, together with two of their big guns, it cost us dear, for at nine on Tuesday morning we had only sixty-five men left.'

Private T. Ackerley; 'Old Boy', June 1915.

CHARLIE W., AN "OLD BOY" IN THE NAVY, WILL FIND HIS FAMILY GROWING UP ON HIS RETURN.

DADDY," CHARLIE W. WENT DOWN WITH THE "HAMPSHIRE."

The cost of war: these two pictures appeared in successive copies of the Society's magazine in 1915.

First World War. Driver E. Read (above) stands for his portrait before moving to France while from the Senior Service an unknown old boy stands to attention outside the Waifs and Strays headquarters at Old Town Hall, Kennington (facing top left).

Below: Second World War. (Left) leaving his London Home a boy scans the sky for signs of a raid, (centre) a brother and sister, their destination and name labels neatly tied to their coats stand outside the station waiting to be evacuated to the country; (bottom) An evacuation party leaves its city Home; when the children return after the war some Homes will have been razed to the ground, others left filthy and ramshackled after being commandeered by the forces. Nevertheless Home staff would labour night and day to get their Homes back into working order after the war.

By the end of the first war there were 1,444 men from the Homes of the Society in the army or navy and 126 had been killed. The conflict had brought a new crop of 2,179 children for the Society to look after.

Twenty-three years later the story is told again. Over five hundred old boys actively engaged on the battle fronts, admissions to Homes up from 1,000 a year to 2,699. But there were two new developments—evacuation and war nurseries.

As soon as war was declared the Society was ready to move its children out of the bombing zones. When the first air raid warning sounded, on September 3, the children were 'out of town'. It was a wise precaution. In the first three years of war more women and children were killed in bombing than soldiers killed in action. Safe they might be, happy they were not all. 'I always remember poor little Jill who used to cry to go for a walk round Woolworth's because the peace and the beauty of the countryside was so strange to her. Children don't appreciate the countryside, nor do they enjoy long dreary walks in it!'

Many of the new Homes in the depths of rural England belonged to the aristocracy who took a lively interest in the children. 'It was His Grace this and Her Grace that and then we had to say our own grace at meals, the children were very confused.'

Refugee children and mother from two world wars. Right: A continental family consider their bleak future now their home has been destroyed. (Below right) A bombed out mother accepts a cup of tea as her children sit bemused beside her and the welfare adviser discusses what to do.
(Imperial War Museum)

Below: The result of a raid by four FW190s which attacked a Kent town at roof top level. Five of the household were killed.
(Imperial War Museum)

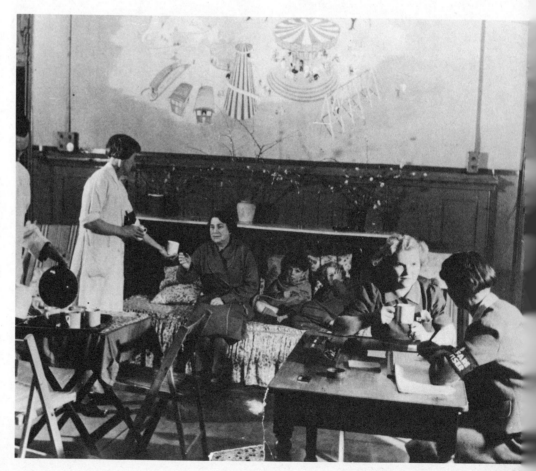

Left: Children asleep behind netting in a Hampstead nursery and (below) far from the terrors of war evacuated children run freely in the Devon countryside.
(Imperial War Museum)

Different styles in residential war nurseries.
Facing page, bottom: a brother and sister
being cared for at a day nursery in Surrey,
probably Kilronan which was supported by the
Junior American Red Cross. Food, clothing
and cash from the New World was a major
factor in maintaining the health of the
evacuated children in the Homes and
nurseries.
Facing page top: A Children's Society war
nursery at Wendover, Buckinghamshire. It
was the policy to board out children who had
come into the nurseries with foster parents
after the age of five.
(Imperial War Museum)
Right: The Beatrix nursery, Handsworth,
Birmingham: lots of staff, lots of uniforms,
nursing care excellent but a bit formal for
modern taste?

Matrons opened their doors to slum children who had been evacuated and then turn
out of their billets by their new guardians. 'I little dreamt,' wrote one owner of a coun
mansion, 'that English children could be so completely ignorant of the simplest rules
hygiene, and that they would regard the floors and carpets as suitable places upon whi
to relieve themselves.' The national evacuation of three and a half million women a
children in 1939 revealed to an incredulous middle class the extent of deprivation th
still existed in the cities and helped fuel the call for a new charter for children.

For those mothers who could not get away, war nurseries were set
throughout the country—the Children's Society providing a quarter of them. They we
nearly all dismantled after the war and never again have so many women been so free
pursue their own careers unhindered by the daily responsibility of their children.

Food, clothing and toys poured in from the International Red Cross and fro
the 'Lions' in Canada. In some Homes the introduction of rationing meant a disti

improvement in the quality of food—at last there was a widely recognised minimum level of nutrition against which to plan the daily menu.

The children came into the Homes at the rate of five a day—some were unable to walk or speak because of shell shock, others had been badly mauled physically by the bombing.

'Jill was six years old in January. Her father was drowned at the evacuation from Dunkirk and her mother was left to care for Jill and her two younger sisters and brother. They were bombed out of their home in 1941 and their mother, who was never very bright, has become more and more demented and the children more and more neglected. The mother had several times threatened to destroy herself and the children. Jill and the other three children are now settling down in our Homes.'

'Small John, who is two, came to us at the age of sixteen months having had pneumonia, whooping cough and measles in his short span of life. His mother, who was expecting another baby, was bombed out of her London home and went to the west; there she suffered further raids, and when her baby was born she gave up the unequal struggle and died, taking the new baby with her. John and his older brother came to us, and John is now rapidly losing all signs of his unfortunate beginning in this world.'

One boy was discovered living with his ailing grandfather in a deserted house. The old man slept on a pile of coats on the floor, surrounded by baked bean tins he used as chamber pots. When the boy was brought into the Home he was lousy. 'He always had an odd smell about him even after a bath,' a matron recalls. Fixed up with new clothes and new boots he went to bed with his boots still on—they were his first pair and he would not remove them for fear of someone stealing them. 'We needed his ration book to feed him so we had to go to a brothel in Bristol where his father was living to cajole the book from him.' Years later, when his parents decided they wanted him back he refused. 'I don't know you,' he told them to their face.

The same phrase was heard from countless children returning to their hard working parents as the war ended. For staff, parents and children it was a very painful time.

Top: A brisk walk by the sea; sea defences against possible invasion would have made the beach less than inviting, (bottom) growing your own food was essential to eke out wartime rations. That marrow looks as if it's on its way to the village fête!

Facing page top: A British Tommy in the First World War looks after two children made refugees by the advancing troops *(Imperial War Museum)* and (below) Canadian troops stationed in England during the Second World War pose with some of the Society's children after the soldiers redecorated their Home.

Matron may have looked severe but most were prepared to work all hours God gave them for the children—and by no means every child would have been better off fostered or adopted.

Love

When all is said and done this is a tale of love, sometimes misconceived, mixed up or muddled, but recognisably love; the attempts of grown-ups to help children in need.

'The head matron (who was the cook when I first went in the Home) had tears in her eyes as she bade me goodbye. I couldn't understand why her voice was broken as she told me to be a good girl and look after my father. I was soon to find out how much I missed her and the other girls.'

So much love. At Christmas time in one Home the floor of the sitting room is covered with the sleeping bags of old boys returning to their home. The utter dedication of countless staff. One matron who kept her own home in London open for old girls to visit was killed in the blitz as she was entertaining some for tea. Others would work long into the night stitching and mending or preparing the Homes for a celebration. They worked for decades for very little money; they had little life of their own. Their own children were brought up with the children of the Homes; deep and lasting friendships were struck up between child and child and between child and adult.

'At the time it seemed they were an awful lot, but as I got older I realised that they were very kind and considerate.'

'So many staff keep leaving. I find it hard to form a long-term relationship because I know they will eventually leave, so many have. The hardest time was when my houseparents left when I was thirteen. I had grown to love them and they just left.'

'I think there should be a time stating how long houseparents should stay.'

As Homes have become smaller, more like families, so have changes in staff become more frequent. Is it fair that such close relationships should so easily be broken?

There have been three answers to the frustrated love of children unable to be sure that those they love will not go away, fostering, adoption and keeping the child with his own folk.

All are far more difficult to 'see' than a Home. If they are a success—and so many children have grown happy in such care—then the child is absorbed into the community, with no way to tell he was once a 'waif and stray'. As always it was the failures that were noticed. Our friend the Rev. Charles Whitaker, writing at the turn of the century waxes lyrical about fostering.

'I could take you to the country where, amidst fields and gardens there are whitewashed cottages close to an ancient church. In one of these cottages I could show you a child to be proud of, a child with a pretty, rosy face and sweet long-lashed eyes. The happy little face and obvious affection between the child and its foster mother will tell you all that you want to know about her present condition.'

But it was not always like that. A cripple recalls her childhood in Leicestershire in the thirties: 'I was boarded out with a woman who needed someone to fetch and carry. She had arthritis in her legs and I would get the water from the village pump—I was nine at the time. I would fetch two pailsful and it used to hurt my legs. I would do her shopping and all the cleaning. I used to black lead the grates and the big range. I was always getting smacked with a stick. I don't think I was all that naughty. When I was thirteen I complained to the schoolmaster and showed him my arms which were very bruised and then I was taken away to a Home.'

'I am convinced,' said one senior member of the Society, 'that there are a lot of deeply hurt children who cannot make the close relationship with foster parents who are happier in Homes where there are not the high emotional demands made on them.'

Right: One of the Society's oldest Homes, in Dulwich, with the children packing the windows—the caption on the back of the original photograph reads 'With love from the children, May 1930'.

Below: A foster mother with her three foster children in the 1930s. For many fostering was the chance of a real family life and the basis of their future happiness.

Inspectors were brought in by the Society to ensure the supervisors, usually the local parson, lady of the manor or a retired schoolteacher, were keeping an eye on the children in foster homes. By the end of the last war these amateur supervisors were phased out. 'The foster parents were ordinary folk in my area,' recalls one inspector, 'farm labourers and factory workers but deeply committed to the Society. I was not able to get around during the war but afterwards I did not find one child who had been ill treated.'

But the foster parents were as diverse as the children. 'They were good fun at first, but when you really got to know them they were too upper class for me—I was that much different,' said one fostered child.

Adoption was another way to answer the child's deep need for someone to call Mother. How many times a day will a four-year-old call out for his mother? Forty, sixty times in a day—for those with young children it is a test worth making. Then listen to the children in a Children's Home and make the same test. Not often, perhaps not once.

Houseparents in their love for the children understand this longing and in their unselfishness many have pushed the Society to seek more adoptions.

One young teenage girl suddenly couldn't stand being with her friends any longer. 'They get all the boys when we go out dancing,' she complained. Asked why she wanted to leave her friends she said: 'I just felt I wanted to run far away because I was adopted.' Twice she became hysterical and had to go to hospital. 'I had a blackout when I remembered I was adopted.' Slowly and carefully a helper explained to her her background, why she was adopted and what had happened to her as a child and as he did so she grew calm.

And there is a third way. Little Peter is two and his mother is seventeen. She lives at home with her parents in their two-up two-down house and Peter screamed all day, everything he seized he broke and at night there was still no peace. His young mother was at the end of her tether and it looked as though her child would be taken away.

Instead mother and child have been visiting one of the Society's day centres each day where they both can find friends and space to relax. At first Peter was pinching and punching but now, if he sees another child cry he will go over to comfort him. His mother sees a future for them both, she is learning to trust others, cope with her own parents and take responsibility.

Ways of expressing love for children in need have changed as the children and our understanding of them have changed. The new 'waifs and strays' are now rarely orphans, nor are they likely, as their forebears humbly and gratefully to submit to being helped. They may be difficult, sometimes deeply disturbed, they may indeed be effectively homeless, eking out an existence with their mother in a bedsitter which acts as nursery, kitchen, laundry, living room and sleeping quarters all rolled into one; they may be aimless and workless teenagers or children whose parents are both at work when they return from school; they may be the children of lonely and isolated families in England's sterile new housing development.

'Why has God implanted in us this beautiful gift of compassion and love for little children? Is it that we may be touched for a moment by some piteous story, and go on our way and forget? Is it that we may indulge ourselves with the delights of well cared for children, while thousands are left to want and misery? No; surely God means that our love and pity should go forth in action and should steer us to self denial and generous aid for the helpless.' The Rt. Rev. William Walsham How, first chairman of the Executive Committee of the Waifs and Strays.

What's it like outside? A boy writes home in 1955, his battered bible a rest for his note pad—and his thoughts? and (facing page) a teenage girl considers her future.

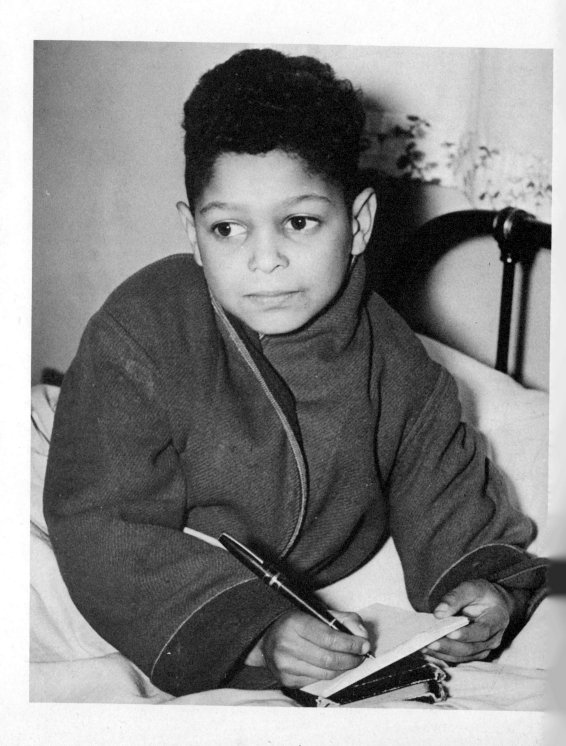

Today's children are different—and they are allowed to express themselves in a way unthinkable a few years ago. Right: a teenage boy and teenage girl's room in a special unit in Southport. Selfconscious the pictures may be, but they are a measure of the change the Society has had to face.
Facing page: How it was. A bedroom at St. Francis Home in West Sussex, September 1939.

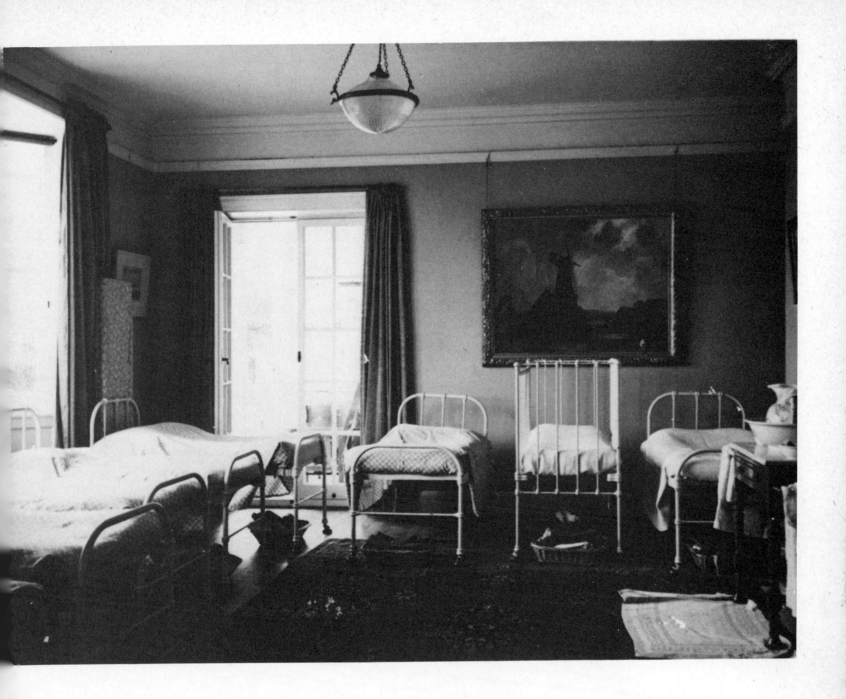

These children cannot be ignored and society sleep comfortably in its bed any more than could the original waifs and strays. To quote from the Children's Society's 1896 report, as relevant today as it was then: 'It is surely right for the Society, acting in the name and on behalf of the National Church to come to their relief . . . and help them to keep their homes together and maintain their independence.'

Love demands that the children are listened to—it is what they want that must be taken seriously not what is convenient for grown-ups to provide for them. By not listening to a child an adult with the best intentions in the world can make the worst mistakes. Putting children first is as much a challenge for the Children's Society now as it was when it first set out in faith one hundred years ago.

The dingy slum streets have given way to brave new towns, there is more space—but often more loneliness as parents are out at work and the old family structures continue to crumble. To take the children away would only accelerate the social decay—family centres, such as the one sheltering behind the block wall at Milton Keynes are being set up to support parents and children while they remain within the community.

Acknowledgements

Many people and organisations have been involved in helping to bring this Centenary book to fruition and to them the Children's Society here records its thanks. Amongst them the Society particularly records its appreciation and very sincere thanks to Patrick Walker the Chairman of Watmoughs and to its Directors for their generous gift in printing this book without charge: also to Feldmuehle (UK) Ltd and R. A. Brand Ltd for supplying the paper and to Lorilleux & Bolton Ltd and Fishburn Inks Ltd for supplying the inks.

The Society also records its thanks to George Rainbird for his initial support and advice and to Sir John Betjeman for writing the foreword and showing such interest in the project.

Many of the photographs have been sent to the Society by Old Boys and Girls and ex-members of staff and to these we acknowledge our debt of gratitude and also to the Trustees of the Imperial War Museum, to the Merseyside Maritime Museum and to the Provincial Archives of Alberta, Canada, for allowing us to publish photographs from their collections free of charge.

The author would like to express an especial debt to John Stroud whose extensive research for his book Thirteen Penny Stamps on the Society's history provided an invaluable fund of material from ex-Home children on which to draw and to Phyllis Harrison, author of The Home Children and to her publishers Watson and Dwyer Publishing Ltd, Winnipeg, for permission to use material from her book relating to Homes children in Canada.

My thanks to the Children's Society staff both at headquarters and in the field for the time and help they freely gave, to the Chairman, the Hon Mark Wyndham who conceived the idea of the book, to Winifred Stone the deputy Director who nurtured it and to Mildred and Dorothy Rudolf for welcoming me into the family and tradition of the Society and allowing me to read the Rudolf diaries. Finally my thanks to all those who have written to the Society to tell the story of their time in care and provided such a rich seam of experience from which to mine this Centenary book.